West Coast Impressions

West Coast Impressions

THE DYNAMIC BRITISH COLUMBIA LANDSCAPE

Photography by Paul Gilbert   Text by Kathryn Graham

RAINCOAST BOOKS

Vancouver

First edition published in 1992 by Wild Light Press

This edition published in 1995 by
Raincoast Book Distribution Ltd.
8680 Cambie Street
Vancouver, B.C. V6P 6M9
(604) 323-7100

CANADIAN CATALOGUING IN PUBLICATION DATA

Gilbert, Paul
West coast impressions
ISBN 1-895714-68-0

1. British Columbia – Pictorial works. 2. Landscape – British Columbia – Pictorial works.
3. Photography – British Columbia. 4. Landscape photography.
I. Graham, Kathryn. II. Title.

FC3812.G54 1995   779'.36'711'092   C94-910844-8
F1087.8.G54 1995

Printed and bound in Hong Kong

*This book is printed on acid-free paper produced from selectively harvested trees. No clearcut, rainforest, or
other endangered-species products were used. The manufacturing process involves
no dioxin-producing chlorine.*

This book is dedicated to those who have the foresight to
fight for the preservation of wild places

Contents

Sunset colours and a lone hiker linger as the crescent moon sets in the west (*title page*).

The outgoing tide reveals the domain of inter-tidal life at Schooner Cove, Pacific Rim National Park (*preceding page*).

Sunlight penetrates the morning mist, Carmanah Valley (*left*).

The Coast Mountains recede into the distance while rolling waves advance upon the shore.

Preface

What draws us to the edge? What attracts us to the place where land ends and water begins?

The intensity of life along Canada's West Coast is a major part of its appeal. Plants struggle to establish themselves in the sand and to survive the salty air and the harsh wind. The rise and fall of the tides creates a severe habitat for inter-tidal plants and animals. They must survive not only the pounding of the waves when the tide is high, but also the drying effects of wind and sun when the tide is low.

Here, too, we find some of the forms of life most revered by humans. Who is not thrilled by the sight of the majestic eagle watching over its kingdom? Who does not stand in admiration of thousand-year-old trees that dwarf humans?

Then there is the water, that huge restless body stretching from coast to horizon. The water that carves the contour of the landscape, that carries microscopic nourishment, that fills the air with ethereal mists. The abundant precipitation produces the conditions necessary for the lush rainforest growth. Standing in the silence of a coastal cedar grove, one can sense, indeed almost hear, the burgeoning of life, so great is its intensity.

Paul and I are drawn to the West Coast for all of these reasons and more, for it also offers lighting conditions ideal for photography. Sunrise finds us at the beach, a rocky headland, or a mud flat in hope of capturing the delicate colours. As the sun burns away the morning mist, a unique type of lighting occurs, creating a radiant intimacy that Paul loves to use in his photography. On damp misty days we go trekking through the rainforest or exploring tidepools. The glittering light of a sunny day, or the subdued light of a brewing storm, offer other possibilities. Sunset can present a palette of soft pastels or a dramatic display in the sky. Often we linger long after the sun has set, watching the sky and the water to see the variations produced by the fading light, the emergence of the stars and the setting of the moon.

Over the years we have seen many changes. Although the wilderness seems immense and everlasting, in reality it is vulnerable. Every year the unspoiled areas become smaller, more fragmented, and more precious. So as well as singing the praises of the wild West Coast, this book is an appeal for its protection.

Colour

Ocean blue   Blue sky

Forest green   Green moss

Sunset yellow   Yellow lichen

Lily orange   Orange glow

Paintbrush red   Red berries

Fireweed pink   Pink dawn

Seastar purple   Purple dusk

The West Coast's palette of colour is endless and ever-changing – there are a million greens in a rainforest, and no two sunsets are ever the same. Whether subtle or spectacular, these colours are influenced by the different kinds of coastal light.

Clear sunny days offer deep blue skies and glittering waves. Moist overcast days present the rich saturated colours of wildflowers and forests. Sunrise and sunset display all manner of warm hues in delicate washes or bold strokes of colour.

Indian paintbrush create a splash of colour among beached logs.

The setting sun silhouettes a hiker (*above*) and fills the sky with vibrant colour in the Coast Mountains (*right*).

3

Lupines and Columbia lilies make a delicate display on a mountain slope (*left*).

The brilliant blues of a sunny day at Florencia Bay, Pacific Rim National Park (*right*).

The waters of Kennedy River (*above*) and Carmanah Creek (*right*) flow jade-green as the first buds of spring appear.

The lush growth of an ancient spruce grove displays a multitude of greens – everything from moss-green to fern-green to leaf-green.

Such stands of Sitka spruce are found in coastal river valleys where trees can grow to over 3 metres (10 feet) in diameter and to over 85 metres (278 feet) in height.

On Vancouver Island only 1 out of 90 watersheds is completely protected.

Starbursts of green stand out against the autumn forest floor (*above*), like the brilliant
blooms of salmonberry against alder trunks in spring (*right*).

Fireweed (*right*) and Indian paintbrush (*far right*) dominate the summer splendour of a mountain meadow.

A young swimmer dashes exuberantly into the cold Pacific Ocean.

Presence

Electric encounter

Distant kinship

Silent spirit

Powerful presence

Ancient energies

Sweet surprise

People, animals, plants, or objects observed or encountered often colour our impressions of a landscape. Whether hoped for or unexpected, momentary or unhurried, the presence of these things evokes an emotional response – of awe, of delight, of affinity, of reverence.

Black-tailed deer abound on the Queen Charlotte Islands. Less than a metre tall, these deer were introduced to the islands and flourish without natural predators.

Timeworn totem poles watch over the ancient village of Skedans, Queen Charlotte Islands.

Diminutive monkey flowers cling cheerily to rocky cliffs near the ocean (*above*).

The setting sun illuminates the fluid contours of a sandbar (*right*).

Motion is ever-present in the West Coast landscape – a bald eagle in flight (*above*)
and the roll of a windswept wave (*right*).

Green blankets a boulder in the inter-tidal zone (*above*).

Tiny blood stars sparkle on the wet sand (*right*).

Forest

Towering trees, tiny fungi
    Life pushing up, decay breaking down
        Swirling pulsing growth, hushed cathedral
           Moist air, misty light, mud underfoot

A thousand years pass,
This verdant world is ever-changing, never-changing

    Green
        Green
           Green

Walking into an ancient rainforest is an amazing and awe-inspiring experience. The magnitude of the trees, their venerable age, never fail to impress. The timelessness of their world is rare and profound. But the trees are just one part of this dynamic ecosphere. Countless others are equally important: everything from bunchberries, ferns, and moss, to mushrooms, slugs, and squirrels play a role in the ongoing drama of life, death, decay, and new life.

The author contemplates the uncommon occurrence of the Triplets, Carmanah Valley.

Backlight shows the brilliant mood of a sunny morning in the coastal rainforest (*above*).

The airy pattern of a fern contrasts with the massive trunk of a cedar tree (*right*).

Ancient rainforests consume vast amounts of carbon dioxide and produce large quantities
of oxygen – one hectare gives off more than 13 metric tonnes of oxygen a year.

Ocean mist drifts through the temperate rainforest, Queen Charlotte Islands (*left*),
and essential moisture is combed from the air by evergreen needles (*above*).

Like living candles, yellow skunk cabbage glow in the dim light of the forest floor. The bright blooms are seen in many wet areas in early spring, and the huge leaves last throughout the summer, lending a tropical flavour to the temperate rainforest.

Clusters of red bunchberries punctuate the greenness of the forest understory (*above*).

A hiker is dwarfed by immense trees in an old-growth forest (*right*).

Soft light filters in among the stunted growth of a spruce fringe forest (*above*).

From the decaying mass of a huge stump springs new life (*right*).

The elegant beauty of bunchberry dogwoods is sprinkled among ferns (*above*).

A winding trail leads through groves of towering Sitka spruce in Carmanah Valley (*right*).

A moody sky hangs over Green Point, Pacific Rim National Park.

Edge

The restless ocean
        The ebb and flow
Tides rise and tides fall
        Sun rises and sun sets
Land meets water
        Ocean meets forest
Vertical encounters horizontal
        Endless beaches, infinite sky

Although an edge is often thought of as a definite line, on the West Coast it is an indeterminate expanse where different forces converge. The interaction of these elements creates an atmosphere of energy and change: constant motion, shifting moods and colours, fluid coastal light.

A red rock adds a dash of colour to a cobble beach (*above*), and Indian paintbrush emblazons a weathered log (*right*).

Low tide exposes purple seastars, sea anemones, seaweed, and barnacles to view (*above*).

The incoming tide surges over mussels and barnacles on a rocky headland (*right*).

Weathered branches cling tenaciously to life on an exposed cliff (*above*).

The ebb tide reveals the preponderance of a boulder on the beach (*left*).

Looking toward Vancouver Island
from Clayoquot Sound, with Meares
Island dominating the view.

Inter-tidal life encrusts a seemingly inhospitable point (*above*).

Lichen traces a lacy design across a seaside rock (*right*).

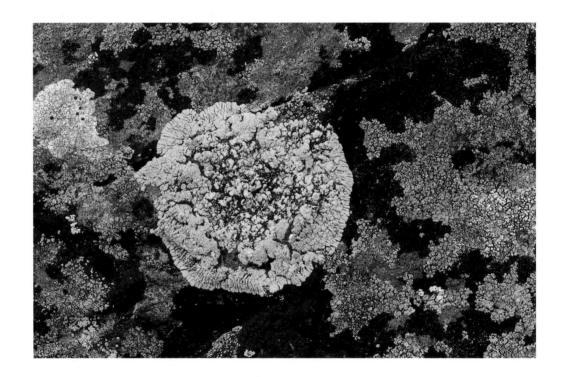

Waves crash and flow continuously, in, over, and around the rugged coast (*above*).

A couple enjoys the twilight glow along the edge of the ocean, Pacific Rim National Park (*right*).

Morning light catches a feather as it rests momentarily on a ripple of sand.

Light

Morning Light, evening light
Sharp light, sparkling light
Soft light, liquid light
Pure light, delicate light
Intimate light, eloquent light

To create a photograph is "to write with light." Therefore the most essential tool for photographers is excellent light – light that reacts dynamically with film to produce images that are expressive.

The changing atmosphere of the West Coast creates a variety of lighting conditions, each revealing a different facet of the coastal character, from bright sunny days to moist moody mornings and tranquil evenings.

As the morning sun burns off mist, an eloquent light is created – in a subalpine forest (*right*) and along the coast (*above*).

The subtle colours of sunrise (*left*) and sunset (*above*) are captured through long exposures.

Soft light accentuates colour and form to produce images that are full and refined.

61

The twilight glow, from both direct and reflected light, paints a vivid portrait of Long Beach, Pacific Rim National Park.

The rich greens of the temperate rainforest are produced by moist, penetrating light.

The rosy warmth of the setting sun colours the evening clouds and touches logs on this Vancouver Island beach.

Photography

The first time I visited the West Coast of British Columbia I was captivated. I fell in love with the endless beaches, the windblown salt air, and the towering primeval forests.

The second time I returned with childlike enthusiasm and a keen desire to capture this spectacular landscape on film. The results were disappointing. Like many amateur photographers, I felt bewildered by f-stops, shutter speeds, and light meters. Rather than an extension of my vision, the camera was a barrier between me and my interpretation of the landscape.

As a student of photography, I learned more about camera techniques and visual design. This newfound visual literacy enabled me to see more clearly. However, the connection between what I saw and felt and what I tried to express still didn't translate onto film. In time I discovered that for me to communicate successfully what my mind's eye perceived I had to begin thinking in the language of light. I learned that making fine photographs depended not only upon being enthusiastic and connected to what one is photographing, but also upon understanding that light interacts with film differently than with the human eye.

The word *photography* can be translated as "writing with light." Whereas I used to search primarily for composition, I now go chasing light with a better knowledge of how film responds to it.

In photography classes and workshops I stress the importance of "writing with light." I encourage students to experiment with a variety of film types, then to choose one or two films and get to know them intimately.

One of my favourite times of day along the West Coast is long after the sun has set. Working near the edge of the ocean under low levels of direct and reflected light can produce rewarding results. Here, where our eyes see little detail, film can respond to subtle yet rich qualities of light and colour through long exposure. Several photos in this book were made at this time of day, using exposures ranging from one second to five minutes.

I strive to elicit a more visceral than intellectual response to my images. As a landscape photographer, I seldom include people or wildlife in my work. The dynamics of West Coast light, colour, form, and pattern provide me with ample photographic opportunity. However, on occasion the juxtaposition of something living and the natural landscape can enhance visual harmony and effectively communicate my innermost feelings.

The driving force behind my photography is the need to discover more about the world around me and to express clearly how I feel about it. I hope that the photos in this book will serve as a collective reminder of how essential it is to preserve remaining wilderness ecosystems and old growth rainforest watersheds in British Columbia.

— PAUL GILBERT

The lush colour blanketing the forest floor is a patchwork of multiple tones of green.

Technical Information

Due to my photographic style and the transient nature of light, I use equipment that allows me to respond quickly to changes.

When making the photographs for this book, I employed both 35 mm and medium-format systems. I find the Pentax 6x7 to be the camera best suited for most landscape work. It provides me with the same quick response of a 35 mm, and with today's fine-grain films, quality approximating that of a large-format camera.

The photographs in this book were made with either Fujichrome Professional 50 or Kodachrome 64 film. I prefer Fujichrome for forest photography, due to its capacity to record every nuance and tone of green, and Kodachrome for its ability to register accurate colour, especially in direct sunlight.

Polarizing filters were often used to reduce contrast caused by glare and to increase colour saturation. A tripod and cable release were utilized when necessary to avoid camera shake and to facilitate the use of small f-stops to maximize depth of field. And finally, when printing this book, great care was taken to preserve the integrity of the original scenes.

— PAUL GILBERT

Special thanks to our families and friends for their patience and support.

To inquire about photographic workshops, hiking tours, or the
purchase of photographic prints, contact Paul Gilbert at:

135 — 4800 No. 3 Road, Suite 125

Richmond, B.C.

V6X 3A6

A shutter speed of one-quarter second is used to depict the delicate cascades of a waterfall (*above*).

A five-minute exposure captures bands of colour not visible to the human eye (*overleaf*).